CIRCLE OF FRIENDS

The ultimate secret to choosing the right friend circle

ALEXIS J COATES

© **Copyright 2022 by Alexis J Coates**

All rights reserved.

This document is geared towards providing exact and reliable information with regards to the topic and issue covered. The publication is sold with the idea that the publisher is not required to render accounting, officially permitted, or otherwise, qualified services. If advice is necessary, legal or professional, a practiced individual in the profession should be ordered.

- From a Declaration of Principles which was accepted and approved equally by a Committee of the American Bar Association and a Committee of Publishers and Associations.

In no way is it legal to reproduce, duplicate, or transmit any part of this document in either electronic means or in printed format. Recording of this publication is strictly prohibited and any storage of this document is not allowed unless with written permission from the publisher. All rights reserved.

The information provided herein is stated to be truthful and consistent, in that any liability, in terms of inattention or otherwise, by any usage or abuse of any policies, processes, or directions contained within is the solitary and utter responsibility of the recipient reader. Under no circumstances will any legal responsibility or blame be held against the publisher for any reparation, damages, or monetary loss due to the information herein, either directly or indirectly.

Respective authors own all copyrights not held by the publisher.

The information herein is offered for informational purposes solely, and is universal as so. The presentation of the information is without contract or any type of guarantee assurance. The trademarks that are used are without any consent, and the publication of the trademark is without permission or backing by the trademark owner. All trademarks and brands within this book are for clarifying purposes only and are the owned by the owners themselves, not affiliated with this document.

Table of Contents

Introduction 5

Chapter One 8

What Is a Circle of Friends 8

    The Different Types of Friend Circles 10

    Who is in Your Inner Circle 15

    The Importance of Friendships and Friend Circles 17

Chapter Two 20

Effect of Having Negative Circles 20

    Evaluating Your Friends in Circle of Friends 24

    The Second Tiers of Friendship 27

    Understanding Family Circles 28

Chapter Three 32

Friends Circles in Sport 32

    Understanding your Social Friends Circle 34

    Keys To Increasing Your Social Circle 36

    Business Social Network Circles 40

    How to Maintain your Business Social Network Circles 43

Chapter Four 46

Planning your Future Circle 46

    How to Make Future Circles 48

    Mixing Circle of Friends 52

Keys to Mixing Stronger Friendships Circle 54

Circle of Influence Friends 56

How Your Circle of Friends Influence Who You Become 58

How to Expand Your Circle of Influence 60

Chapter Five **64**

Understanding Money Circle Friends 64

    Things to Remember When You Hang Out with Money Circles 65

    Don't Cross Circle Lines 69

    Advantages of Having a Big Circle of Friends 70

Chapter Six **73**

The Development of the Social Self Environment - Keeping Friends.. 73

    Types Of Friends You Need in Your Circle 76

    Benefits of Having Good Circle of Friends 78

    Reasons Why Circle of Friend Makes You Healthier And Happier.. 81

Chapter Seven **85**

Keys to Making a True Circle of Friend and a Better Relationship.. 85

    Signs of A Negative Circle of Friends..................................... 87

    The Secret to Choose Your Circle of Friends 91

    Ways To Manage Your Circle Of Friends and Have The Best Relationships 96

Conclusion **99**

Introduction

The individuals in your "circles of friendship" are those who are close to you, who have a thorough understanding of you, and whom you can rely on to always be there for you in times of need.

I've found that people can make friends in various ways as adults. People you meet at work, friends of friends who have been introduced to you at some event, people you attend workshops where you meet like-minded people, getting involved in hobbies, or volunteering for charity work instead of complaining conceitedly about not having friends because someone out there needs your help and who knows what friendships might form.

Then it is up to you to create the circumstances for the growth of such friendships. These can include organizing a support group, having lunch with someone, etc. I'm trying to convey the point that we frequently assume, as adults, that we won't make new acquaintances, yet this is not always the case.

You deserve to have a diverse circle of friends because every friendship is unique. You can think of your friendships as a group of circles that fit inside each other. People you like but don't know well are in the outermost circle. These are people you've met at work, church, or other gatherings, as well as friends of friends and other friendly acquaintances.

Some of these people are now the closest they've ever been to you. However, some of them go into the next circle and get closer to you. These are people you like a lot and visit frequently. They could be transitory buddies who matter to you at the time but don't stick around.

Or they might be people you go out with but aren't close pals of yours. It's worthwhile to try to become closer to a casual buddy if you're truly fond of them. Invite a stranger to coffee or cigars after a meeting or to a party at your house to let them know you'd like to get to know them better.

Your relationship can progress to the third circle, which is making friends. You'll both take advantage of the chance to get to know one another better and determine whether you share many interests. With considerable work and good fortune, the friendship might finally advance to the fourth circle, which is reserved for close friends. A relationship typically takes some time to progress to this point, but once it does, you will both have a lasting bond.

Friendships are the best way to enrich life. You likely recall the proverb, "Keep the old friends while making new ones. A silver one and a gold one." You come to realize how true this is as your life progresses. You can ensure you receive your fair share of joy, support, and company if you have many friends nearby.

Everyone has different types of people in their life. There are relations, friends, coworkers, acquaintances, and colleagues. There are also different degrees of closeness within each of these circles. For instance, you might feel more comfortable and connected to one sister or relative in your family than another.

Or, within your circle of friends, some can be significantly more dependable and friendly than others. Some coworkers may be true friends even in the workplace, while others are less close. The degree of distance or intimacy that will be effective in these relationships depends on their differences. It will be really different if you can tell the difference between different levels of friendship.

Chapter One

What Is a Circle of Friends

Living a happy and fulfilling life requires having strong, healthy relationships. Your relationships with other individuals can range from those with whom you are very close to those with whom you only have passing acquaintances. You can gain some insight into the kinds of limits you might wish to set by being aware of the various circles or levels of friendship. The "best friend" you should share your most private thoughts and feelings with is not just anyone.

Consider the many degrees of friendships you may have had throughout your life if you are unsure of the status of your relationships. The next three levels of friendship are explained in detail. Then, choose where your current friendships fall in your life.

1. Your Inner Circle

- Your closest friends should be modest, rarely more than five, so that you can always count on them in times of need. You can trust them to always be there for you in times of need since they are very close to you and understand you.

- Surround yourself with the proper people. These individuals will strongly affect you and ultimately affect your feelings.

2. Your Middle Circle

- The middle circle is where you spend most of your time, your close friends. You converse with them about your experiences, interests, joys, and problems. These are the individuals you eat lunch with, sit in class with, laugh with, and enjoy yourself with a round golf.

- Compared to the people in your inner circle, you have a less emotional involvement in this group of pals. Although you might express your opinions, you probably take care to keep your innermost feelings and thoughts to yourself. These buddies are vital to your life, although they may come and go from this circle depending on your shared hobbies, activities, and amount of time spent together.

3. Your Outer Circle

- Your outer circle consists of acquaintances with whom you may or may not have a close relationship. You come across these people very frequently. When you cross paths, you say hello, you laugh together, and you could chat about how your day was or recent development in your life. However, you wouldn't want to reveal your deepest emotions, struggles, or secrets to them.

- These can be individuals you interact with on social media, reside in your neighborhood, or see at school or phone of golf. These are very movable people who will probably come and go from your life over time. Spending excessive time and energy on a person in your outer circle can make you feel resentful, rejected, or ashamed.

The Different Types of Friend Circles

When it comes to starting, establishing, and sustaining friendships, seeing friend relationships as a collection of concentric circles might help us understand the wider picture. A deep friendship is different from a temporary friendship, and relating to an acquaintance is different from relating to a stranger. Friendships don't come in one size fits all.

Every friend group or "circle" has its own set of specific presumptions and restrictions. Knowing these limits enables us to be aware of the ways that friends transition from one circle to the next, such as when casual friends become best friends and when acquaintances develop situational friendships. You can visualize your relationships as being arranged into a series of concentric circles, with you at the center of each one, to get a mental picture of how the many types of intimacy occur in your life. Look at these "circles" of friends:

> Concentric circles are **circles with a common center.** The region between two concentric circles of different radii is called an annulus. Any two circles can be made concentric by inversion by picking the inversion center as one of the limiting points.

❖ Acquaintances

An acquaintance is a person you are only passingly familiar with; they are not friends.

They are slightly more approachable than a total stranger; you might know their name and a few of their friends, but you don't really know them. More so than a stranger, but not as a friend, you know them. Even if you might work or attend the same school as them, you might never speak to them. Even though you may say hello to them daily, you don't have close relationships with them.

❖ Situational Friends

A situational friend is one who hangs out in a certain setting. You interact with situational friends in the setting where you first met, such as school, the workplace, or an area of interest. What unites you is the particular setting or area of interest. The friendship ends till you next meet each other when the "situation" changes.

❖ **Casual Friends**

A casual friend is more than just a situational friend but not yet a close or "best" friend. They are likely your friends, and you enjoy spending time with them because you have similar interests. Depending on your shared connections or interests, you might occasionally run into them or hang out in a group. They might be a brand-new friend that you're only getting to know better. By sharing interests, you have fun while also fostering a relationship founded on mutual respect and understanding.

❖ **Best Friends**

The "best" friendships are those that are based on honesty, trust, and of course, shared interests. They need work from both sides to maintain and are built over time. Our close friendships offer us a wealth of advantages and are immensely satisfying. Because of the level of emotional intimacy, we can develop with these people, close friendships can feel like families.

But developing strong connections requires time and effort; it doesn't simply happen. You might begin as one of the aforementioned types of people and end up being great friends.

❖ **Circumstantial Friends**

These might be neighbors, coworkers, parents at your child's preschool, or folks you enjoy chatting with at the gym cigar lounge even though you don't know them well personally. These people are amiable and practical for doing specific things together (for instance, a coworker with whom you eat lunch), but the friendships don't persist if the circumstances change (you change jobs or move away). A circumstantial friend may occasionally progress into the third circle or even closer by becoming a personal friend.

- ❖ **Self**

We may not first consider ourselves "friends," but to form relationships, we must be aware of who we are. The center of the concentric friendship circles is always our individual selves. What interests do we have? What causes happiness in our lives? What are our partnerships' strong points and weaknesses? How can we treat others with kindness? How do we show friendship? Humans, by nature, require social interaction. Positive prosocial activity is what keeps each of our personal buddy networks connected. A warm grin fosters a prosocial mindset and conveys to people that you are approachable and eager to make friends.

There are various levels of privacy required in each of these circles. The people you are most comfortable being personal with will be included in the innermost circle, for instance if you carefully selected who to let in.

These are the people you confide in and share your innermost thoughts, secrets, sexuality, and home with (just how close you get depends on your personal preferences and on how considerate and caring they are).

The level of intimacy and disclosure of your private self-decreases with each subsequent circle. For instance, a new coworker in the outermost circle will likely be familiar with generic facts about you and little about your personal life.

These social groups are adaptable; acquaintances can develop into temporary friends in certain circumstances, and casual friends can elevate to closest friends. While friendship circles are constantly evolving, the true friendship requires two people, time, commitment, trust, and honesty.

Being friends is a decision. And when making friendship decisions, we must hone our perspective-taking abilities to judge whether the other person wants to be our friend. The advantages of having friends exceed the difficulties of forming connections, even though it might be scary and seem like a lot of work.

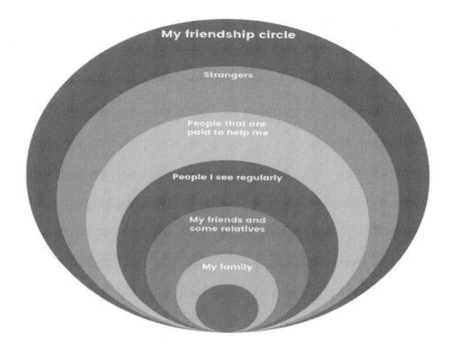

Who is in Your Inner Circle

Even if they do not use the same network, many mobile phone providers now boast about your inner circle and offer discounts or free minutes for connecting with them. This offers something to ponder.

We frequently like the five people we spend the most time with. What comes to mind when you consider your inner circle? Who are the five individuals you talk to, confide in, like being with, and reach out to when you want to celebrate and share your successes and struggles?

Consider each of these individuals. What life lessons are they imparting to you? What kind of mentoring do they provide? Do you feel that being around them has helped you grow? If you were a fuel tank, would they fill you, or would anyone ever empty you, even only occasionally? What do you provide them in return? Do you fully respond, satisfy their needs, and be present when they call?

Why are they a part of your close circle of friends? What makes them unique? Are there any shared traits amongst them? What principles do they follow? Do they match your own?

How recently did you express gratitude to them? What are you occasionally doing to impress them, like your most discerning clients? What do you have that maintains you in their sphere of influence?

If you can handle it, broaden your thinking a little bit more. Take a look at the outside limits of your inner circle. Are there any individuals who are merely on the outskirts who would desire to enter? Is anyone trying to catch your attention, perhaps?

Is there anyone who wants to enter but cannot get past the barrier guarding your closest relationships for whatever reason? Do you want to invite somebody who is just out of reach inside? Maybe a person you spoke to at the gym or a new neighbor who seems like they could develop a close bond.

What about a coworker who admires you and wants to ask you to be their mentor but is too shy to do so? Are there those on the periphery who somehow managed to leave the circle but found it difficult to re-enter because of their busy lives?

Finally, do you need to take care of the version of yourself that is on the outside circle? Perhaps due to a hectic lifestyle or job schedule, people have less time for enjoyment, self-awareness, and relaxation. How can you make it a priority to take care of yourself?

Take note of the circles you have around you. You might even consider widening your inner circle to include more people; don't worry, it won't increase your communication plan's costs. Make the modifications you deem necessary. Share your gratitude for your supporters, consider inviting new people, and consider removing any if required. Let's consider the happiness that comes from being able to interact with others as humans.

The Importance of Friendships and Friend Circles

Friends enrich life, whether they are new friends, old friends, or closest friends. Not only that, but they also bring to the partnership their distinct personalities and backgrounds. But also because of all the advantages that friendships provide and how those advantages might alter us.

Without my pals, I find it impossible to picture my life. Watching them is a pleasure because they are all unique and special in their own ways. We can converse for hours about business, fashion, or our families or ask our best girlfriends for guidance on a personal issue. They cheer me up, they make me smile, and they share their life with me. A friendship's resilience might be severely tested by time and altering personal circumstances, but the ones that last have strong roots. Using this checklist, consider your friends' contributions to your personal journey and acknowledge them. A circle of friends provides us with:

1. A feeling of unity. We all desire to blend in and form connections with people since we are social animals. A method to connect with people who get us and give us the freedom to be ourselves is through friendship.

2. Help when you need it. When we cannot function due to personal trauma, such a major sickness, friends provide a sympathetic ear. Many times, all that is necessary is for someone to truly listen.

3. A new viewpoint. It's not always simple to take a step back and think straight when faced with a difficult issue. When that happens, a friend's "outside" viewpoint can help us see things differently and more objectively.

4. An increase in confidence. When our confidence is being battered, we can all use a cheerleader (or three). Friends that genuinely care provide us encouragement and words of wisdom to help us get through those temporary setbacks.

5. Willingness to adapt. In particular, best friends can act as role models. They can motivate us by demonstrating the power of a good outlook and taking action to complete even the most difficult tasks.

6. Health advantages. People having a broad social network outlived people with the fewest connections by 22%. It serves as evidence of how friendship might lessen anxiety and despair.

Chapter Two

Effect of Having Negative Circles

"Respecting yourself doesn't mean you have to hate others; it just means you have to cut them out of your life." Not everyone is intended to remain. When you were seven years old, friendship seemed much more understandable than it does now. As you get closer to being a young adult, you realize that making friends or rather, keeping friends is more difficult now than it was when you were a teenager.

Your circle of friends gets smaller, and you can count how many of them you genuinely trust on the one hand. You begin to lose connection with your former friends and feel quite insignificant compared to your new friends. Really, it's a pretty awful scenario.

Some people can now face the facts of the situation. A small percentage did, however, try harder. Now, trying harder is a noble action since it demonstrates how much you appreciate friendship. But you must understand that some friends are not worth the trouble. In actuality, it is detrimental to your health.

- ❖ **The friend you shouldn't trust**

If your friend consistently implies that you are to blame for everything, it may be time to call gaslighting what it is and go on. If someone is treating you poorly while professing their love for you, pay attention to their behavior rather than their words.

When you explain why you were offended when someone stated your new dress would look better on them, they can accuse you of being overly sentimental and nasty. If they repeatedly indulge in these behaviors and then blame you when you try to address them, it's time to return your friendship card.

- ❖ **The companion who is unrespectful of your boundaries**

Even though you've informed them you're going to bed if you have that one friend who always Face Times you late at night, they might not be respecting your limits. It can be necessary to take the risk of first explaining and then upholding your boundaries to your buddies.

Being that vulnerable emotionally can be daunting, but you need to let your friend know that even though you generally enjoy physical contact and hugs, crying makes you uncomfortable being touched. (Yes, they probably ought to ask first and touch second, but communication happens both ways.)

Setting limits early on in friendships might be the difference between having a good, healthy relationship with someone. Being vulnerable to connecting with another person in a healthy way requires being open and honest about who you are and your boundaries.

- ❖ **Your friend who never contacts you**

When your friend does return your texts (which does not happen frequently), you are the one who always makes the decision to hang out together, so it always seems as though they are doing you a favor. Yes, I suppose supper on Friday will work for me. I anticipate arriving a little late. And I have to leave early, too. Is that also cool? You have the right to request better communication if it seems all too familiar.

- ❖ **The circle of friends who don't value your time**

I'm not referring to the friend who experiences chronic pain and occasionally needs to cancel plans due to a flare-up. I'm referring to the friend who consistently arrives three hours late without messaging or apologizing or the friend who frequently forgets to confirm or cancel plans, leaving you wondering what's going on all the time. You truly can raise the bar, so you don't need to engage in that game of limbo.

- ❖ **The circle of friends who evaluates your objectives**

Your friends will correct you when you're wrong, but there's a big difference between how you feel when your best friend offers you sound advice (even if it's hard to take) and how you feel when a friend criticizes your goals and aspirations. Reality checks are frequently necessary, but you'll know you deserve more considerate support if the response to your huge desire, why would you want to accomplish that?" or "I mean, I guess if you really want to."

- ❖ **The circle of friend you have when it's convenient, but not always**

Even if they haven't talked to you in months, it's conceivable that they are now single or traveling through and in need of accommodation. Whether you feel like they're not exactly using you but are just a substantial presence in your life when they don't really have anything else going on, it's reasonable to start to wonder if you really need them in your life.

- ❖ **The circle of friends who only shows up when they require something**

They may text you or visit you frequently enough, but they only seem to be truly there with you when they have a need.

You always appear to be there for them when they need to rant about the ex they saw over the weekend, but they never seem to have time to help you when you need assistance handling a work problem of your own. More reciprocity than that is due to you.

❖ **The companion who betrayal your trust**

You want to be able to talk to your best friend about the fight you and your partner had, including where you may have gone wrong. They assured you that the chats would stay confidential, so you naturally anticipate this. But you'll definitely be rethinking what to discuss with them in the future when you learn that you're being a complete jerk in your relationship from the cousin of a buddy of your best friend's roommate (if you two have a future at all).

Evaluating Your Friends in Circle of Friends

According to some, choosing your circle of friend is crucial to your success, and the friends you keep now might be a strong predictor of your future success. What type of network do you have for support? Do the people you call friends truly care about you? Are you pushed to improve by them? Are they mental challenges? When situations are bad, are they there for you? Are you among them? When thinking about your pals, these are excellent questions to ponder.

We can keep our lives peaceful and in balance by maintaining genuine friendships. There is no greater reward than having friends you can rely on, trust to be there for you when you need them, and who let you into their lives.

Are your friends adding or removing value to your life? Do your friends hold you responsible, encourage your aspirations, pray for and with you, and are open and honest with you even when it hurts? If not, you should reassess your interpersonal connections.

We select our friends and romantic partners depending on how we feel about ourselves. What would you say about your friends' circle? Take stock of your situation, decide whether it benefits you, and if not, make the necessary adjustments. Assessing your relationships with friends is critical to ensure they're solid and fulfilling.

1. Is it only because it's convenient that I'm friends with this person?

Convenience is among the primary motives I've observed for maintaining friendships. Perhaps you've been friends with someone for a while now after meeting them at work or in a class. Although living nearby someone is a great reason to develop friends, it is not a good one to keep those friendships going.

2. Do they positively impact my life in any way?

When assessing one's friendships, this question is essential since we frequently grow accustomed to someone treating us a certain way and subsequently find it difficult to identify that their actions are not beneficial to us.

Consider the favors you and your friend provide one another when assessing your friendships. Maybe one of you listens extremely well, and the other has fantastic counsel. Or perhaps the two of you are adept at helping each other out when they require it. I frequently witness people having a detrimental effect on their friends, such as coercing them into doing things they don't want to, acting rudely, and pointing out flaws in them.

Although I firmly believe in the need for self-improvement, I begin to question whether a friendship is healthy when someone offers criticism as advice. Since friends are supposed to build each other up, you may want to reevaluate your friendship if you feel like your friend only ever uses your weaknesses against you.

3. Do I envision a long-term friendship with this person?

You might be looking for friends for various reasons, depending on your life stage. In high school, you usually want to hang out with fun individuals, whereas in college, you're looking for your "people."

Being able to keep your best friends and coworkers apart in the workplace may be something you enjoy. yet, regardless of your situation in life, it's still necessary to be selective about your circle friends and decide if you want to keep them as friends for the long term.

You must put forth effort if you want to maintain your friendship with someone you made friends with in college out of convenience. The relationships that you actively seek out and work to develop each day are the best.

Be careful how you let someone impact your life if you only consider them as a temporary friend. You shouldn't tell someone all of your secrets simply because you've had a few enjoyable nights with them if you don't entirely trust them.

It's never too early to practice how you can determine if someone is a true friend because we all desire those lifetime pals at some point. You may make sure that you have supportive friends nearby who will support you through all of life's ups and downs by giving meaningful friendships a high priority. Developing and preserving a strong friendship is necessary for a friendship to flourish since it takes two to tango.

The Second Tiers of Friendship

Friends who become close to you for that time are known as second-tier friends. This may happen because you work together, attended college together, or connected at that stage of your life. These friendships may or may not last after the current circumstance changes, the moment passes, and you go on to your next stage of life.

That doesn't mean the friendship dies or there is hostility; it's just that it isn't a top priority for you any longer. You might maintain the friendship in some form, but only when you can, and you won't really feel awful if it stops. They aren't usually around, even if you enjoy hanging out with them and you do have some things in common.

You very well may have a few second-tier friendships—that is, friends by connection rather than necessarily by choice—in your community, school, or place of employment.

Your circle of friend shrinks as you get older, which is wonderful. Along the way, you begin to identify the friends that are not just supportive of you but also share your viewpoints. With these friends, you start to enter a judgment-free zone where you may fully be yourself.

Not everyone does, even if it takes time and good fortune to build that kind of friendship. Additionally, you end up with many transient friends who support you during that period of your life. The friend you met on your solo trip to another country who joined you on those sightseeing outings, or your professional colleagues who have become friends but with whom you tend to lose touch when either of you leaves the office. These friendships might not last very long, but they are important now!

It can be challenging to make friends at any stage of life. While friendships can occasionally be difficult, there are moments when you meet someone, and there is an immediate spark of understanding between the two of you—or even more in a small group.

Understanding Family Circles

Have you ever convened an "emergency family meeting"? Were you seated around the kitchen table in a circle? Or crouch on the couch together? How did that meeting come about? There's a good chance that the situation or conflict wasn't ideal. It might have been a missed curfew, difficulties in the classroom, or a rude outburst. We come together, start discussing, and solve difficulties when we are faced with family challenges.

What if, on the other hand, your kids connected family circles with open, cordial, and supportive communication? Issues, but also!

This go-to system preserves and supports family discourse, builds a strong foundation of trust, and promotes genuine connection since family systems continuously change as people grow and adapt. By employing this technique, you and your family will develop positive associations with sitting in circles and conversing about various family-related issues. Your kids and teenagers won't view "circles" as a lecture or a punishment during the "meeting," but rather as the fertile ground where the family raises its children in love and understanding.

No beginning or finish can be found in a circle. Making eye contact with everyone in the circle is possible because each person's seat is equal to the next one. Family circle participants all occupy chairs or floors at the same height.

This represents shared and equal power. Each family member has the freedom and room to express themselves, as shown by the circle, which denotes that all family members deserve the same respect. Having a structured conversation while seated in a circle is referred to as a "circle" as well.

The talking piece is a piece of equipment that may be passed both safely and easily. It implies that only one person will speak at once and that everyone else will pay attention while the speaking member is not present. Focus, endurance, and turn-taking are encouraged because the talking piece always moves around the circle in order, regardless of whether a participant chooses to skip a round. A talking piece can be produced or chosen to follow the subject of each individual circle, or it might be something that the family values and can relate to.

A complete circle turn is referred to as a "round." The topics covered in family-building circles are frequently pre-planned and narrowly focused. The family is led through deliberate discussion and sharing by a series of questions. Each family has an equal chance to speak and be heard because the talking piece controls the round.

Your values serve as a guide for how you think, feel, and act. What do you think matters the most? What is important to you? As a guide for how you will interact with one another during the circle process, family members identify their values (and move forward from the circle). The dialogue and the interactions are also guided by values, which define safety rules.

Family members participate in each circle equally, although one family member may serve as the facilitator for a certain circle. The facilitator reads every prompt and ensures that the circle's rules are followed. Children can take on leadership roles within their families through facilitating.

You will see increased trust, communication, and openness when you use circles frequently to create a family community. Then, when conflict develops, you already have a method and connected emotional history for dialoguing about how to change and mend the damage.

Chapter Three

Friends Circles in Sport

A wonderful technique to meet people if friends are what you're looking for is to join a sports team. Sports-related activities have helped to create a lot of initial friendships. An excellent method to meet new people is to participate in school athletics.

You need to trust one another when you and your team are working together and following the same set of rules. You may play to each other's strengths as you grow to know one another. This is a great approach to increase the bond between you two.

Sports have the ability to unite a wide range of people and can serve as a bond between your circle of friends. You must interact with your teammates while playing as a team, which might be a little method to strengthen the link between teammates.

This will guarantee that you have more following the practices, improving both your understanding of the sport and the thoughts that the other person has. Sharing private information, as a result, can help people become more than just passing acquaintances.

You'll come to appreciate the advantages of allowing others the opportunity to demonstrate their own talents when you and your friends participate in a sport. When it comes to forming friendships, all of this is valuable.

In life, we all look up to others. Young children's parents are responsible (which parents can never get enough of in the younger years). But as kids become older, they start to glance down more often than up.

Young adults look to their friends, acquaintances in general, or members of the expanding circle of friends who affect them. Sports, or more specifically, engagement in sports, is one area where friends can have a significant impact. Being a part of a circle of friends can affect one's sporting experience.

A young person's involvement in sport is significantly influenced by their friends' participation, which has positive effects on their mental health, young people benefit the most from extracurricular activities like a sport when they engage in them with peers from their social networks.

This is because the presence of friends in a team context is essential to the positive effects on self-esteem brought on by sports engagement. To put it another way, having a close group of friends is linked to having higher self-esteem and a better view of yourself in sports.

So, when it comes to sports, a child's peers, who they look up to in their adolescent years, can have a significant and inspiring impact on a child's engagement in sports and what they take away from the overall experience.

Even team-based sports like tennis or golf, which involve partnering, can strengthen already-existing bonds and foster more cooperation among small group members. The objective of joining a sports team is to play fairly and treat other players with respect, whether they are on the same team as you or not.

Finding their areas of weakness in this way may enable you to occasionally assist them in strengthening those areas. One of the best methods to form a lifelong friendship is through sports, which may also result in strong relationships off the field. Additionally, it is a great method to meet new people. An incredible technique to form strong ties with a group while socializing.

Understanding your Social Friends Circle

At least not seriously; we don't care who we hang out with or what we do. The value of social friends nowadays is not only undervalued but also gravely misunderstood. Most of us define a social circle as a group of acquaintances with whom we hang out, with whom we connect, with whom we are close, and with whom we first connected well and now frequently interact. Is this how you define a social circle, by any chance? If the answer is yes, you clearly don't understand what a social circle is all about.

The most fundamental principle of a social circle is to get together and do something innovative or beneficial. You have a great social circle if you indulge in a leisure activity every weekend that relieves your tension and, in turn, allows you to master a new skill or passion with a select group of people. It's also a terrific idea to have creative discussions over beverages!

Today, a social circle or a place where certain individuals of common interest meet and eventually become friends cannot be described as only a group of close friends. Social circles have drastically changed in recent years, and as a result, we now belong to numerous social circles rather than just one or two.

You can discuss all of your issues and solicit advice from numerous people at once on a social circle's platform. Sometimes we want to talk about a certain topic with people who are not involved in it, and a social circle gives us the opportunity.

People in your social circle won't be biased because they aren't your closest buddies. Similar to this, there are instances when you develop an interest in a new topic, such as current events. You probably can't talk about that at home, but you can when you get together with some friends for drinks. Sometimes, all we need is for someone to affirm that our actions and thoughts are correct. This is something that a social circle not only ensures for you but also respects you for. It kind of serves as motivation as well.

Keys To Increasing Your Social Circle

The concept of a true friend has virtually little value in today's culture. It's fairly usual to listen to song lyrics or watch television where friendship is continually criticized and undervalued. You may have witnessed or heard about close friends betraying or abusing one another, and everyone appears to believe that everyone else is a "fake."

Even though it can be challenging to meet true friends, you don't have to spend your days feeling depressed and alone. Today at work, a coworker underlined the value of someone simply being present no matter what during a chat. Even though being there can make all the difference, we are frequently too preoccupied with ourselves to notice when those around us need us.

It's okay to be friendless. Loneliness can be brought on by relocating to a new city, making lifestyle changes, or having significant arguments with a close friend. You might always meet new people.

You can do a variety of things to broaden your social life, which can significantly impact various parts of your life. From a personal and professional standpoint, deciding to expand your network can be very gratifying and fascinating. What, therefore, can we do to broaden our social circle:

1. Engage with others!

This can happen to the postman, customers at the bar, or even passengers on the train (which occasionally results in some strange reactions!). However, conversing with individuals about relevant topics will typically make you appear outgoing. Being approachable is crucial to this process; therefore, strive to adopt an affable stance and perhaps even an approachable appearance.

2. Start a new interest

As you share a shared interest, having a pastime is a great way to meet new people. For the more daring, a wide variety of pastimes are available, including photography and pole dance classes. Making new acquaintances is more likely when the activity is more interesting. Try to consider topics in which you are genuinely interested before looking for classes in your area.

3. Go to conferences and gatherings

This may be a fantastic approach to making new friends. I continue to believe that you never know how someone could be able to assist you. I've found that sometimes the people you least expect.

4. Networking events

This can be a terrific method to expand your social friend, but they can also be a great place to meet new people.

5. Make an effort to establish a pattern in your life

By doing this, you'll be far more likely to meet new people and develop friendships with them. Even if you only nod hello, it doesn't hurt to say hello to someone you recognize!

6. Even basic activities like exercise might result in new friendships

If you join a gym or even go for a jog on the same circuit, you will undoubtedly meet a few individuals before long!

7. Locate others who share your interests

You can do this by looking through websites devoted to a specific subject or activity or by consulting your local newspaper. There will undoubtedly be several events advertised that you have not thought of.

8. Sharpen your social skills

You must figure out how to maintain stimulating and constructive conversations. Asking a lot of questions is a crucial part of doing this. Expand your horizons and try to develop an interest in what others have to offer. Once the initial themes have been established, you can continue the conversation by posing further queries.

When you come across subjects that really interest you or about which you are well-informed, be sure to keep the conversation intelligent. People enjoy responding to those with whom they connect.

9. Create a social network

Making friends is a skill that may be acquired. People and things both undergo change. You need to develop your ability to adapt to others around you. Try to stay in your area of interest and look for groups that share your traits.

Additionally, it's crucial to hold off on making snap judgments and go a little deeper to learn more about people. It's possible that you share more things than you think. If you happen to click with someone, schedule additional social time with them throughout the week.

You'll gradually start interacting with more people who share your interests, and they'll probably introduce you to their friends and acquaintances. The trick is to keep the relationships strong once you've established them. Bring your new circle of friends together once you've made a few.

Let them engage so you can form your own group. Your group will start to come together, enabling you to communicate, make plans, and have fun together.

Finding new friends can often be a slow and gradual process, but there are fun and interesting individuals out there who you might want to get to know. You just need to look for them. I wish you luck.

Business Social Network Circles

Social networking is no longer simply for youngsters to use for entertainment. It is an excellent tool for networking, connecting with lucrative people, and fostering professional ties.

Social networking is the process of interacting with and connecting with social circles and groups, which may one day aid in the expansion of an organization. Social networking is the practice of maintaining contact with friends, family, coworkers, customers, or clients using Internet-based social media platforms.

It's a big duty to connect with people who share your interests and aspirations, have experience in your profession, or are possible customers. This type of marketing is quite powerful and may be utilized to attract plenty of clients. But many people who utilize social networking to grow their businesses are doing so entirely in the wrong way, which may not be understood.

Social networking is NOT the place to advertise your company, goods, or content. You will fail if you use these tools for this purpose, which practically everyone does. You won't just fall short; you might even harm your online reputation. Building business relationships is the purpose of social networking.

It establishes your brand by allowing others to learn about you and your goods or services. They find out on their own what you have to offer. You establish connections with individuals and let them learn more about you. Because of the nature of syndication, people become familiar with your name and brand.

While creating your professional network may be the most exciting aspect of this process, it is not the most crucial. Like in business, it's much simpler to attract new clients than it is to keep existing ones' content.

You need to find ways to reach out to be a meaningful connection for someone else. You should consider how you are making the relationships you have worthwhile for everyone involved. You must comprehend how to communicate with others in your network. The only person who can speak to them daily maybe you, yet you may not be able to.

To be clear about what a networking relationship with you will entail, first consider what you can achieve in a reasonable manner.

How much free time do you have? Building your network circle isn't something you can assign to someone else, which hasn't been discussed yet but should be now. Even though you might be tempted to delegate some work to a helper, you risk losing out on the relationship and the knowledge of your contacts if you're not the one talking to them. Consider how much time you can actually spend networking instead. Then, decide which networking occasions or websites are most significant to you, and mark those events on your calendar.

❖ **How many networking groups may you join?**

Even though it might be tempting to join every group out there, it is best to focus your efforts on a few areas. You could eventually be able to increase your capability, but in the meanwhile, concentrate on the websites that are most important to your sector and be active there.

❖ **What kind of networking do you prefer?**

Try to identify your preferred strategy and style. For some, this can resemble being a social media user—someone who is always posting content and igniting debates. Others may discover that you have a personal connection with people and enjoy learning more about who they are and what they do.

❖ **What are your objectives for networking?**

Additionally, you might want to consider your long-term intentions and ambitions. The easier it will be for you to turn the proverbial networking wheel, the more clarity you can provide regarding your direction.

This is a great approach to get the conversation about what you can do going, even though the answers to these questions might alter over time. Once your activities are under control, you'll be able to see what else might fit in, if not now, then later.

Through websites like Facebook, Twitter, LinkedIn, and Instagram, among others, social networking can serve a social purpose, a business purpose, or both. Social networking has become a key platform for marketers looking to engage customers. You must broaden your social network to connect with the most individuals possible to accomplish your goals.

How to Maintain your Business Social Network Circles

Social networks let you connect with almost anyone you've ever encountered, including classmates, coworkers, relatives, friends, and other acquaintances. It's a terrific location to network and promotes your business.

Global relationships have become more accessible thanks to the Internet, mainly social media. Keeping in touch with family and friends who live elsewhere in the world is no longer difficult. A worldwide society with billions of virtual residents has emerged from social networking sites. One of the world's biggest internet communities (more than China's population!) is Facebook, which has 2.4 billion users. Just recently, both on a personal level and in terms of commercial contacts, our world shrank and became more approachable.

1. Keep up with them

You must be willing and ready to speak with the individuals you know to develop any relationship. Though the word "often" may imply different things to different people, it's crucial that you get in touch with your network regularly, such as on the first of the month, every two weeks, Fridays, etc. Don't change your behavior.

2. Inform them about your professional developments

Give a brief overview of your professional situation or objectives when contacting your contacts. Aside from that, you can offer details about any accomplishments and successes you've had.

3. Engage in conversation with them

These connections aren't only about you and your past accomplishments. If it's suitable, inquire about the other person's personal life and professional employment. To determine if they might be able to assist you or whether you might be able to assist them, you want to learn as much as you can about them.

4. Schedule one-on-one conversations

You may want to schedule conversations with your network's connections sometimes, especially the high-value ones. You can establish a closer bond with them if you do this. Seek out time with them if they're attending a professional event. Attempt to arrange a meal if you are in the region for other business. Your bond will become stronger the more times you can get together.

5. Share resources or information that is relevant to their aims

If you learn of something that could be useful to someone else, you should let them know about it. By doing this, you'll increase the connection's overall worth. Using email or normal mail, you might give them book, facts, etc. The other person will be made aware of your thoughts about them and will be reminded of the importance of your relationship in their lives.

6. Compile data on each connection in a file

It is a good idea to gather details on each person you interact with when building your network. You'll start to notice trends in who you speak with, who has offered you assistance, etc., by creating a dossier of your connections. The holes in your network will also start to show themselves.

7. Comment on their updates, profiles, and comments by reading them

Always read the posts, comments, and other content on their social media or networking profiles. As a result, the individuals in your network will feel recognized and valued and will repay the favor.

Your connections will do more for you due to your interactions with them and your efforts to make them feel valued. You can discover that some of your contacts are not as active as others, it's true. At this stage, you may want to focus on contacts replying and returning the favor.

Chapter Four

Planning your Future Circle

Humans are social creatures. We can't endure being by ourselves. Nearly of the time, we require someone to be by our side. In our happiest moments, we need people to laugh with us; in our saddest moments, we need them to weep with us. And we are among the luckiest individuals on earth if we are fortunate enough to be in the company of some very nice and devoted circle of friends. True, only the most fortunate people have friends who are devoted to them and always by their sides.

A buddy is someone exceptional you can spend your whole life with, even if they are not a member of your family, are not related to you by blood, and do not even share a family or a home with you. Even when you want to cry, they can make you laugh. They are the ones who will do whatever to lift your spirits and help you get through your worst moments. Let us discuss good friends' positive effects and influences on one's future circle.

You begin to perceive yourself as deserving of love and grow more at ease with loving and affirming yourself as well the more people you have in your life who openly love you for who you are.

"Avoid those who want to minimize your goals. Small people always do that, but the truly great inspire you to believe that you can achieve greatness as well. Have you ever spoken with your pals about this?

Friends play a significant role in our lives; some of us even serve as family. They are not only the individuals we spend the majority of our time with, but they also have the most in-depth knowledge of us. True friends use this information to lift us up, but some friends use it to tear us down.

Everyone runs into issues. Everyone experiences sadness and loneliness from time to time. If we have good friends with whom to discuss our issues, they will never allow us to lose hope or perish in despair. A wonderful companion may lift our spirits like joyous medicine. People tend to make the worst choices if they have no one to talk to during difficult times.

A true friend aids in your safety while you navigate the difficult patches. If someone is present to prevent you from making poor judgments during difficult times, your future will undoubtedly be secured.

No matter how difficult it is, good friends never lie to you. They will never encourage you if you are acting badly and will stop you without worrying about how you will react. They might advise you to start studying if your examinations are coming up and you are wasting time. If they notice you acting up around your parents, they will be the first to ask you to apologize. They will always be upfront with you, no matter how tough it gets.

Good friends help you change who you are. They have a very positive impact on your future circle. They will give you the world's best speech if you need some inspiration. They are the ones who will become aware of your detrimental behavior initially. Your buddies would never leave you alone if you run into problems.

How to Make Future Circles

One of life's most crucial elements of happiness is having friends and meaningful relationships. It's arguably the most crucial factor in determining our general happiness and well-being, aside from our health. A few crucial techniques to remember can significantly enhance your future circle relationships and your physical, mental, and spiritual health.

❖ **Constantly strive to connect with others**

Sharing an emotional experience with another person is the foundation of a connection. This implies that you provide stories about your life and inquire about theirs while you are speaking to someone. Discover your commonalities, your similar hobbies (so you can connect over them and pursue them together), and your unique life objectives.

Next, consider if there is any way you may use collaboration to broaden your impact, support one another in achieving your objectives, and produce something you can be proud of in the future.

- ❖ **Keep in mind that despite our differences, we are all the same**

You should get to know people beyond their outer look since everyone you meet has experienced experiences that you haven't. Everyone is a unique personality, and they all have something to learn from them that can help you live a better, happier life. What you learn from others can also be passed on to help others.

- ❖ **Keep in mind that you have something unique to contribute**

You, too, have had a special set of experiences, just as we can learn from others. You can recognize that you are a special person with a lot to offer the world that others can't, and you can concentrate on using what you've been given to create something wonderful for the world that no one else could possibly create—something that is wholly an expression of YOU—once you get in touch with your core self, embrace who you are, and feel at ease in your own skin.

❖ **Always be authentic**

Many of us look with envy at specific parts of other people's lives and wish we had their wealth, good appearance, or popularity. Given our current circumstances, we assume that having this one thing would make us happy or fulfilled, but we fail to realize that we all have a unique instrument to play in the orchestra of life. By pretending to be someone else and not being ourselves, We're like a round peg trying to go into a square hole.

And if we'd be willing to play our instrument instead of someone else's, we'd be able to tap into our own special abilities, passions, and skills and be able to offer the world something that no one else can because of our special combination of knowledge and experience.

❖ **Always leave a positive legacy wherever you go**

You do not wish only to be born and pass away. Set as your top priority, figuring out how you can make a difference and do something unique that will change the lives of millions of people just because you were born. In the end, what you leave behind is the only thing that will provide for people after you're gone.

You want to come here, showcase your individuality, learn, and develop, and use that unique experience to create something that will impact the world long after you're gone, just because YOU were here.

❖ **Don't push things**

I'm VERY enthusiastic about this, and I realize that sometimes it's difficult to accept when things seem to be at their worst. The reality is that unless we follow our circumstances down the road, we won't be able to determine whether they were good or terrible in the overall scheme of things since we are unable to predict how each of our circumstances will turn out in the "grand picture."

❖ **Never attempt to control others**

We say things like, "If he had done that, I wouldn't be so wretched," or "If she had done that, I would be pleased," far too frequently. But in reality, you can only manage how you move your own arms and legs; You have no influence over what other people do, and you can't expect others to do things specifically for you. Nothing else will ever make you happy if you're not content inside.

❖ **Don't pass judgment on others**

If you observe people, you'll notice that they frequently criticize others for what they say or do, even though they themselves are equally flawed and have flaws in other areas that are just as bad. They also frequently try to convince themselves that they are somehow better than others because of the way they view the world.

Do not forget that you are a flawed human being, and as such, you have no right to think of yourself as being in any way superior to others. Furthermore, passing judgment on others fosters hatred and negative energy, neither of which we want to see spread throughout the world.

If you can do just one thing to improve someone else's life, do that one small thing with the next 100 people you encounter, and you've just made a hundred people's day. Always remember that the key to achieving anything is having a simple awareness of how to do it.

Mixing Circle of Friends

Friendships play a significant role in our social life and directly impact how you feel and how you are feeling. In actuality, you might become more upbeat and productive with certain individuals. If you think back to your most recent meetings, you may quickly recognize those individuals.

You should spend more time with those buddies if you return to work or home smiling and in a good mood. So how exactly do you go about assembling a circle of friends who will benefit your life?

Spending time with like-minded individuals is among many people's most crucial well-being strategies. They've discovered that keeping in touch with supporting relatives and friends daily keeps them healthy. They've even discovered that communicating how they're feeling to someone else can make them feel better.

You might believe that there are no supporting individuals in your life or that there are so few of them that you frequently feel alone. You might believe that your isolation and lack of companionship cause you to experience sadness or depression occasionally or frequently. If you live alone, this issue can get worse.

Most people concur that having at least five close friends and support in their lives would be beneficial. Everyone desires and needs friends. They make your life better. They enhance your sense of self-worth and vitality. When you require particular care and attention, friends might be especially beneficial.

You might be able to come up with another fun activity that the two of you might do together. Slow down. This will allow you to assess whether this is truly the kind of friend you want.

And if you "come on too strong," other people may feel threatened. The bond grows as you both start to enjoy one other more. While you are with the other person, pay attention to how you feel about yourself. If you have confidence in yourself, you might be on the right path to a satisfying friendship.

Finding the proper people to hang out with is easy if you consider yourself extraordinarily fortunate to have them in your life. These people will stand by your side no matter what. Therefore, be sure to frequently express your gratitude for their friendship, as doing so will help to solidify your bond further.

Of course, as we all experience various stages in our lives, we don't expect everything to be perfect all the time. Your closest friends should be those who are encouraging, understanding, and positive no matter what. They might encourage you to put more effort toward achieving your objectives and help you grow.

Additionally, you will always have a group of supporters who have faith in your ability. So, if you surround yourself with optimism, your mental health and life's quality will both significantly increase.

Keys to Mixing Stronger Friendships Circle

People with strong bonds with their friends, family, coworkers, and even the neighborhood community tend to live longer, be healthier, happier, and be more content with their lives. A life well lived.

Building solid friendships circle, having a shared life purpose, adhering to shared values and goals, establishing trust, and knowing you can count on others and that they can count on you are more important components of a healthy relationship. It involves engaging in activities with others that produce happy times. It's about acknowledging all of your positives and negatives for who you are.

1. Identify the unhealthy friendships

Spending valuable time with friends that make you feel worn out and depressed every time you see them is not worth it when you lead a hectic life. Of course, not everyone can constantly be joyful and upbeat, but negative friendships will always make you wonder why you even try to keep those people in your life. It's time to move on from a friendship if it is sapping your energies. Most likely, more people in your life demand more of your focus.

2. Improve yourself

Your mental health depends on you becoming the best version of yourself. You will likely draw people who might not be the best influences in your life if you are constantly down. So, begin by altering your perspective on life and start small. Enroll in a yoga class and work your way up if you are out of shape.

If you work out often, your mood will improve, and you'll feel better. Alternately, consider picking up a new hobby or language. Beginning to work on yourself will make you more present in your life, enhancing your current friendships and improving you as a person.

3. Diversify

We tend to remain with the same old pals as we get older since getting new friends might seem like quite a task. But if you want to develop as a person, you should get out of your comfort zone and interact with those around you. You can start a conversation with someone who seems upbeat and entertaining since positive people are everywhere. So, the next time you're in the gym, don't be afraid to approach a friend and start a conversation about exercise.

4. Stay connected

You need to be connected if you want to have a circle of friends. This requires you to be active in the friendship. Instead of waiting for them to call and ask you out, take the initiative and message them when you feel the need to catch a new movie together or even if you need help with an assignment. Spend time and effort cultivating the friendship. Even when things go wrong, be there for them and offer your complete support.

5. Disconnect from social media

It's a great innovation, but it can be stressful. Going offline and hanging out with your friends might therefore be really beneficial for your personal development. Instead of binge-watching a Netflix series, enroll in a class with your friends. You'll be able to socialize, learn new things, and discuss ideas with others, all of which could result in the addition of one or more people to your current circle of friends.

Circle of Influence Friends

Who is a part of your Circle of influence? Who is in your five? You might want to check out the other members of your 5. The five individuals who are closest to you should add value to you. Your Circle should be significant to you in more ways than just financial ones. Do you have someone there for you when things are hard? Failure is not a choice, but failure is real, we all experience failure to varying degrees, some more than others.

Relationships are the most important thing that affects and shapes our lives as humans. Consider the extent to which a particular parent, sibling, cousin, teacher, coach, neighbor, author, speaker, boss, coworker, spouse, or friend shaped "who you are today." Values, behaviors, knowledge, skills, interests, passions, hobbies, tastes, and attitudes are frequently acquired through social interaction.

Even so, most people haven't consciously selected their largest "circle of influence" despite how influential relationships are. Fortunately, or sadly, some people enter our lives by default. Some people are married. Geography is important. A factor is the place and type of employment you undertake for a living. Even friendships grow as a result of external factors. Numerous people who are part of this consortium make up our "circle of influence." While some are harmful, others are merely bystanders; we are frequently fortunate to form enlightening relationships that positively influence our life. How does your Circle support you as you navigate daily challenges? Here are the inquiries you should make regarding your circle of influence.

- What positive, negative, or neutral qualities may this individual bring to my life?
- Does this person bring worth to your life?
- Can I rely on this individual in good times and bad?

- Can this individual motivate you to work more and call you out when you're not being your best?

Your Circle of influence is crucial since, often, this is the group that spurs you on, stifles your development, or both. I've been in several circles in my life, some of which were hurtful to me both personally and financially. Let me be clear: I'm not saying you should fire someone if they can't help you at the moment. I want you to stop and think about where you are.

What person do you spend the most time with? Do they share your objectives? How are they improving you? At some point, we should all examine our circle of influence and ask ourselves these questions. Even if we aren't aware of it, the people we are around can greatly impact us.

You can usually predict how far your life and career will go based on the five people you spend the most time with. I am sure that this is the case. We won't advance if we surround ourselves with people who never criticize us and only praise us.

How Your Circle of Friends Influence Who You Become

Friends significantly impact a person's life. For many people, these are actually unavoidable factors. Many people enjoy spending all of their time with friends. Being with friends keeps us active and young. As a result, we feel mentally renewed and joyful the entire time we are with them. This circle of friends plays a significant role in developing our character. They are the ones with whom we spend the majority of our time.

Our social circle greatly influences how we behave on a daily basis. The choices we make, the plans we make, and the people somewhat influence many other things in our circle. People in a friend's circle will undoubtedly share traits while making decisions, making plans, or even acting in certain ways. Like our parents, our friends play a significant role in our lives. So, keep these things in mind when you make friends and choose people who will help you project the image of yourself you want to have in society. Be who you are, not who your friends want you to be.

❖ **Surround yourself with uplifting people**

Make it a point to only be around individuals who enhance your greatest qualities. Though, you don't have to eliminate someone from your inner circle entirely if they are negatively affecting your life. Instead, be aware that they might unintentionally impede your progress, and take a step back in the relationship.

This may be the difference between reaching your goals and failing to do so. It may sound brutal. Keep in mind that as you move through different life phases, it's normal for your top five to alter and develop.

❖ **Not all criticism is unfavorable**

It's important to remember that if a close friend or family member criticizes you, it doesn't mean they don't like you, it doesn't necessarily mean that they don't have your best interests in mind. Do their remarks have any merit? Can you apply it constructively even if they didn't explain it that way (that's a common flaw)? If you look at it like that, their critique could be a fantastic chance for you to get better.

❖ **Step away from your comfort zone**

Who among your top five circle of influence intellectually pushes you? Anyone? To grow and learn, you must be held to a higher standard. Find them and make a commitment to spending more time with them if you feel that your inner circle is missing that person or those people.

❖ **How do you persuade people?**

Now think about how your actions affect the people in your top five. Are you being as uplifting and motivating as you can? Do you lower anyone else's average? The people who are closest to you must be able to bring out the best in you if you want to obtain the best from them.

How to Expand Your Circle of Influence

We've all heard the proverb that says people judge you by the company you keep. And both in our personal and professional lives, that adage is crucial. It is a proven fact that we let our friends influence us. And because of this, parents will pay attention to the friends their children make; employers will check the backgrounds of job applicants; private schools will conduct in-depth parent interviews before granting admission to their children; private clubs will frequently limit membership to people recommended by existing members, and police will inquire about the victim's social circle when they are looking into a crime.

The main takeaway from the preceding is that your associations will reveal more about you than your real personal actions will, including your ethics, integrity, honesty, basic values, beliefs, and future plans. And you are under constant observation if you are a business owner or leader. Colleagues, customers, vendors, suppliers, and others are all closely observing and paying attention to the people you have power over. This is a significant issue to take into account when deciding who will be in your circle of influence.

We are aware that ending relationships can be painful and challenging at times. This is especially true for long-lasting friendships, coworkers, employees, and other people who have significantly impacted our lives.

As you rise through the ranks of success and leadership, you may find that many of your previous friends and coworkers are not accompanying you on your ascent. This is another aspect of the harsh truth you must face. Various factors will cause some of them to disintegrate and disappear.

Sticking with the crowd that enters a time warp and stops developing is a significant risk to development and growth. You will catch the infection from hanging around with them and may perhaps halt or even stop your own growth. Therefore, you must decide whether to stay in stable and static relationships or move on to others that are more demanding and gratifying. You actually have to choose since you can't have it both ways.

Why would you want to widen your circle of influence and contacts? You must broaden the relationships you value beyond your existing areas of knowledge and strength if you want to advance. Your capacity to develop will increase the more contacts you can make with various people. Here are the strategies for expanding your circle of influence:

1. Get involved with niche communities

Find out where those who share your interests are congregating, whether it's online or in person. You could be able to meet people at mastermind groups, associations, the chamber of business, or toastmasters.

2. Be observant

When speaking with new acquaintances, focus the conversation on them rather than on yourself. It would be wise to work on this talent. People find you more appealing when they perceive value in your presence.

3. Be ready to learn

Enter these new social networks with the goal of picking up knowledge from others. Do not act as though you are perfect or possess all the knowledge. Inquire intelligently and pay close attention.

4. Be approachable

Nowadays, humility is a crucial leadership trait that is rarely discussed, yet being modest and teachable makes you more relatable to others. Authentic people are in high demand as friends and colleagues.

5. Show kindness

Think of yourself as having plenty, and be generous with others. To encourage others' development and progress, share your time, thoughts, and other resources. It's simple to believe that we are too busy to devote time to developing new relationships, but the payoff can help you by enhancing your impact among your circle of influence.

Chapter Five

Understanding Money Circle Friends

What is your financial circle? Or, are you isolated when it comes to taking meaningful financial action? You might not initially require one. We must all eventually scale up, including in terms of our riches. Going it alone is challenging.

Spend time with and make friends with those who have more money if you want to make more money.

It might widen your outlook and boost your income to be around successful individuals. Because we prefer to imitate those we are around, winners are attracted to other winners. Although this is accepted in other circle of society, the wealthy have historically come under fire for their propensity to hang out with other wealthy individuals.

The truth is that millionaires have different perspectives on money than people in the middle class, and there are many benefits to being around them. Most billionaires are unexpectedly modest and don't consider themselves "arrived," which may be even more surprising. Many of them believe that millionaires lack the knowledge necessary to become billionaires.

After all, if someone had the knowledge to make billions, why would they settle for millions? That's why millionaires are constantly working to join that elite club of those who are among the richest people on earth.

How many wealthy individuals do you actually have in your close circle of partners and advisors? Make it your New Year's resolution to spend twice as much time hanging out with wealthy folks.

You might become wealthy if you do this. It is incorrectly taught from the beginning that your circle of friends correlates with your amount of money. Friends who don't talk about money-making ideas with you will either make you broke or won't be able to bail you out if you do. Choose your friends carefully—they will judge your worth. Friendship is like an elevator; you can only go up or down in it. You must thus carefully analyze the friendships you join into.

Things to Remember When You Hang Out with Money Circles

It's challenging to choose to be friends with someone who is wealthier, more accomplished, and more powerful than you. It is a choice since it is up to you whether you want to get along with the individual or not. You were practically on an equal footing financially with your friends and classmates during your time in college.

However, when you reconnect with an old friend after some time, you may find that their financial status is far better than yours. Your relationship may suffer greatly if there is a significant financial discrepancy. When you spend time with the money circle, keep the following in mind.

❖ **Remain honest and distinct**

Money circle friends should be aware of it whether you're attempting to save money for a significant buy or you're just on a restricted budget. When people are wealthy, they find it difficult to manage their spending or say no.

Your money circle can easily splurge if they are unaware of your financial limitations. Feel free to establish and adhere to financial boundaries. If your friends organize expensive entertainment, don't hesitate to provide a more affordable substitute. Your social group will stop pressuring you to waste money once they know your financial predicament.

❖ **Avoid pretending and comparison**

Comparing your accomplishments or success to others is just a lose-lose game. Try to accept the fact that you will encounter people who are wealthier and smarter than you, but avoid doing the same. Comparison almost always causes a sense of hesitation and embarrassment.

Don't focus on the distance between you because doing so will exacerbate it. Consider your own accomplishments and victories instead. Create an attitude of gratitude for what you already have and make improvements.

- ❖ **Access their freedom**

Don't assume that your money circle is being so kind to you out of sympathy for you. Try to imagine yourself in your friends' position so that you might comprehend how unpleasant wealth feels. Most wealthy people make an effort to conceal their possessions.

Take it easy when your companion offers to cover the cost of dinner. Your friend wants to demonstrate that your friendship is more essential than money; it's not window-dressing.

- ❖ **Don't play tit-for-tat**

The goal of your friendship is not to compete. Loyal friends won't complain if you treat them to hamburgers and coke, even though your money circles may be accustomed to fine dining. You are not required to serve a fancy dinner complete with caviar and truffles whenever someone in your circle throws a party with pricey alcoholic beverages and excellent finger foods. They are purposefully and voluntarily generous and kind.

- ❖ **Follow your money circles example**

If you want to learn some effective techniques and become wealthy yourself, making friends with people in the money circle might be quite helpful. By surrounding yourself with wealthy friends, you can eliminate negative money stereotypes, see wealth as normal, and develop fresh financial growth strategies. Unquestionably, the habits of rich and poor people are very different. Of course, I'm talking about wealthy individuals who create their own wealth. Try picking up a few of your friends' routines, and chances are that your financial situation will improve.

❖ **Resist the jealousy**

Being envious of your friends' wealth is a surefire way to sour your relationship and cause it to terminate. If you can't be pleased with your friends, then you aren't really friends; instead, you are frenemies who become embroiled in a pointless conflict. When you hang out with wealthy people and see what they can buy, it can be quite difficult to avoid feeling envious.

You can't tell whether the money makes them happy, though. People who earn more typically put forth more effort and deal with more pressures and difficulties.

❖ **Be proud and confident**

Money circles frequently have various perspectives, viewpoints, and conversational subjects. You could be worried about being ignorant or uninteresting when speaking with your money circles. But your friendship is safe as long as others in your circles are interested in what you're saying.

The sensation of guilt over your income or low-status employment is another negative emotion that emerges when interacting with people in the financial world. But there is nothing to be ashamed of if you work hard to support your family or advance. Remain confident and never consider yourself to be lesser simply because you make less money.

Making acquaintances in the financial world can help you determine whether or not you are happy with your income. If you can't overcome jealousy, channel it for your own benefit. If the amount of zeros in your friend's bank account is still a factor in your friendship, you might want to look for new friends who are not wealthier than you. What about money circles?

Don't Cross Circle Lines

Friends who go too far can cause unpleasant situations. For whatever reason, after years of pushing one other's boundaries, you and your friend have reached the breaking point.

Friendships are essential to our support systems and can significantly impact one's quality of life. Through our companions, we can discover the strength of self-assurance and genuinely develop a correct picture of both ourselves and the outside world. Friends are like a mirror that reflects our true selves and flaws. But these connections may easily become problematic, and it's much simpler to discover them veering toward friendship and betrayal.

You probably believe that is clear, though. Not for all of us, I suppose. Some people have had a lot of traumatic events in their lives and feel extremely ashamed of them.

Some people have experienced so many negative feelings throughout the years that they cannot recognize their personal boundaries. They were afraid to express what they wanted to do, achieve, or say in life, or even say "no" when someone crossed their limits.

They then worry about constantly being hated. Cunning individuals surrounded them. They were raised to believe that you shouldn't express your emotions and that it wasn't important to communicate what you felt. They refrained from acting on their desires because they weren't what other people considered normal. So, they followed what they believed to be socially acceptable. They realize at some point in their lives that that is not what they want to do or say.

Advantages of Having a Big Circle of Friends

When it comes to selecting friends, people have varying criteria. While some people prefer to have a smaller group of close friends, others favor a larger social network. When you have a larger group of friends, you are more likely to have superficial relationships with them because you cannot spend enough time with each of them to form lasting connections. These choices demonstrate the variety of attitudes individuals hold and the effort they make to maintain their connections.

- If you have a broader circle of acquaintances, you are more likely to quickly learn about breaking news concerning events occurring across regional boundaries.

- You have a propensity to stay current on any subject that immediately interests you. To get the specifics of what you need to know, you only need to get in touch with the appropriate person you know.

- You might learn about the place you want to go while traveling. You could prepare in advance with the aid of this.

- If you have a lot of friends, you can take advantage of their hospitality when you travel. Therefore, the bigger the circle, the more chances you can find adequate housing without spending any money.

- You can ask a friend who works in the relevant department for assistance if you want to use some government services. Only if you have acquaintances in your social circle who the government employs is this possible.

- You can ask your friends to help you review the material that was covered during those days if you miss a day or two of class due to illness.

- You can organize activities with your friends' assistance to raise the necessary funds and support for them.

- You can lean on your pals for moral support and ask for assistance when things are tough. If you have the support of friends and family, getting through this tough time will go smoothly.

- Your tight circle of friends will organize funds if you experience a medical emergency and require financial assistance. Naturally, if you receive a reprieve, you can repay the sum.

- To save money on transportation, you can pool your vehicles for everyday commutes to work. This is possible only with friends willing to participate in the circle. You are more likely to find a friend with this mindset in a larger circle.

Chapter Six

The Development of the Social Self Environment - Keeping Friends

Friends are essential for personal growth. Some people believe that your friends mirror who you are, and in some ways, they do. People frequently become friends with someone with whom they share interests, whether those interests are in various sports, music, or even television shows. Many relationships begin with something as simple as a preference for a particular brand of shoes.

However, maintaining the friendship is more difficult because familiarity can occasionally foster contempt. You learn more about someone and yourself the longer you know them. The evolution of a social identity occurs over time and as a result of external factors in the formation of the social self-environment. When important life changes occur, such as moving to a new location or getting married, you could discover that you can no longer easily access your prior network.

Of course, you could always make new friends, but retaining the ones you already have—especially those with whom you may have spent a lot of time and emotion—will help the social self-environment progress past its early stages. Here are some ideas for maintaining long-standing friendships.

1. Attempt to stay in contact

Email is usually a fantastic way to stay in touch if they are far away. With the advancement of technology, online chats are another way to stay current. You can even see each other while conversing.

Connecting online with multiple friends in separate locations to hold a conference call is another simple process. Demonstrate your interest in their lives by paying close attention to their difficulties and listening when they do. You should always be compassionate even if you believe they committed a mistake. If they ask for your opinion, respond politely and try not to appear judgmental. You are not their mother; you are their friend.

2. Show them that you still value them

People you've known since childhood, school, or work are typically considered old friends. Because they have likely always existed, they are frequently taken for granted. You don't really appreciate how much you depended on them for moral support or counsel until they were gone.

Remember crucial details like their children's names and birthdays. Try to set up a meeting if you are nearby, even if it is just for a cup of coffee. When a significant occasion arises, such as a wedding or baptism, make every effort to attend. Inform them in advance and explain if it truly is not possible.

3. Maintain their privacy

Maintain your relationship's foundation of trust. Don't tell anyone, not even your spouse, embarrassing or shameful things about your friends. Although it may be tempting, spreading delicious rumors about your friend will demonstrate your lack of reliability and result in losing an established friendship.

Keep your mouth shut at all times, remain loyal to your friends, and be prepared to support them when they need you.

4. Share with your pals

Sometimes as you age, it seems like you have fewer friends than you once did, and you have a propensity to cling to those who have stayed your friends. When they make acquaintances outside of your social circle, you could feel bad because you think you're losing their friendship.

If you become excessively demanding of their time, they may feel confined and decide to leave the relationship. The best course of action is to strike up a friendship with your friend's pals when the chance arises, such as at a party or family get-together. By doing so, you keep your existing friendships while expanding your network of friends. You never know where or how the best friendships may arise.

Types Of Friends You Need in Your Circle

Friends are absolutely essential! We can genuinely choose this family for ourselves. Some friends truly do stay together like white on rice, contrary to the saying, "There is a friend that sticks tighter than a brother?"

We all require particular friends for particular reasons. A supporter who not only takes our difficult experiences in stride but also offers comfort. Or someone who is brutally honest with us and gives us the truth about what in our lives is broken or needs to be mended. And even a buddy pushes us to our boundaries to bring out the best in us. The list continues. We can all relate to having one friend in our friendship circle that falls into one of the categories listed below.

❖ **The Fun-Friend**

A friend with a wonderful sense of humor has the advantage of seemingly knowing the answers to everything. Even if they aren't making any sense, their humor brightens a tense day and makes you feel better. They are always willing to hear about your issues and vent with you.

They always have a joke or piece of advice to lighten the atmosphere. After speaking with them, you feel like a burden has been lifted off your shoulders. You both use exaggeration to explain specific difficulties in your lives and to make light jokes to lessen your grief momentarily. You both benefit from having the ability to make each other laugh when things are tough.

❖ The Adventurer

Everyone needs at least one brave friend who pushes them outside of their comfort zone. This type of friend exposes you to concepts, ideals, or beliefs you might not otherwise consider. They make you feel less intimidated and more eager to take risks and overcome your worries when they're present. They assist you in drawing up plans for your subsequent stage of development.

❖ The Trainer

You look up to and admire this friend. They motivate you to be the best version of yourself by inspiring you. They act as mentors and make you feel better when you are around them. Because they lead prosperous and content lives, you aspire to do the same. They increase your motivation to accomplish your objectives or, at the very least, to keep working toward them.

❖ The Supporter

This friend won't pass judgment when you have made the worst of yourself. In actuality, he is aware of your weaknesses and would much rather you discuss them with him freely than try to hide them.

Everyone needs a friend that sticks by them even when they aren't feeling their best. However, having someone who cannot correct us when we are wrong is not often particularly beneficial.

- ❖ **A lifter**

This kind of friend sticks with you in good times and bad. Even when it puts them in a difficult situation, they give everything they have money, time, health, and even their lives to make you happy. They are constantly available to help you up if you fall.

They support you and ease your difficulties or discomfort. Most individuals require a variety of friends who can encourage them in various ways, but a lifter is the most exceptional of all of them.

Benefits of Having Good Circle of Friends

Never should making friends include competing with the next person. However, if you're a part of a circle of individuals who are committed to being loyal, trustworthy, and ride or die, you aren't ignoring your hidden blessing. You might think that having your own person exceeds your hopes for the platonic treatment you will receive from the world but go further. You can see the advantages of having a close circle of friends by looking around at your friends since you always enjoy their company.

No one discounts the advantages of having a person in your life, but having a circle of your friends by your side is an unforgettable experience. Although each squad member has a different personality, you all have friendship as a common goal. Each person makes their own unique contribution, which forms a strong, multi-dynamic link. That kind of love is unbreakable.

1. You always have someone's back

In a close-knit circle of pals, support is never far away. Confiding in one person is fine, but it really stinks when you need them there, and they can't be. You can use everyone when you have a strong circle of friends. Can't just one person be there? There are a few others you can call upon to step in.

2. You Can Find Advice from Countless Sources

It goes without saying that you consider the advice of anyone you trust to be sound, but wouldn't having more be lovely? Because each member of your circle of friends is unique, they may each provide you with advice from various angles.

Speaking with other people will help you realize that you might not have considered the situation in that way.

3. You get to be constantly exposed to different personalities

Being around many personalities regularly may sound exhausting, but it actually creates a community of people that is very diversified and unique. You rapidly come to understand and accept that what truly makes someone special is their individuality. These contrasts are what actually enable your circle to flourish.

4. Need assistance? essentially, you have a cheer team

I won't even begin to discuss providing support. Not only are a lot of friends coming, but they are also coming out. They will be the ones cheering you on the loudest in the room. They regularly psych you up regularly, so you can only imagine how hard they'll work when you ask them to do it.

5. Whenever we go out, you're always rolling deep

Being confident means showing up to an outing with all of your friends and taking control of the evening. With them all around, you feel more ferocious and don't mind that there isn't much of a crowd of you. Your crew believes that the more, the merrier.

6. Interacting with multiple people actually takes you to a whole other level

Knowing that a circle of individuals understands you is quite reassuring. More than you and one other person are aware of your concerns, dislikes, and celebrity crushes. You may unwind and continue along a path of authentic expression when you have a circle of friends who actually know you.

7. You understand what family really means

You will learn a lot from your vast network of friends, but they will mostly demonstrate to you that blood relations do not always define family. Together, you guys have created a small tribe that always watches out for one another. I'm not sure what else family really means, if not that.

Reasons Why Circle of Friend Makes You Healthier And Happier

Friends can test us, cause us confusion, and occasionally leave us wondering why we even bother. But just like healthy nutrition and exercise, friendships are crucial to our welfare. Additionally, friendships support our growth as we move through each year of life.

Our school companions show us how to be kind, wait our turn, reach out, and explore new interests. As we enter young adulthood, we get greater knowledge about accepting responsibilities, choosing a vocation, and looking for mentors.

❖ **Friendship boosts contentment**

Even superficial social interactions might improve someone's mood. Any interaction, even with more casual acquaintances, made people happier. Being around happy individuals increases your chances of feeling happy yourself since happiness is contagious.

- ❖ **Your friendships can inspire you**

Humans are social creatures. Thus, we are influenced by the thoughts and deeds of others. It is much simpler to achieve your goals, whether they are professional or personal if your community is encouraging. You always feel disheartened, even if you can usually motivate yourself most of the time. Sometimes just talking to a dependable, sympathetic friend is all it takes to get you motivated again.

- ❖ **Friendship offers psychological support**

Mental diseases like sadness and anxiety affect a lot of people, persons who had close friendships as teenagers have lower rates of despair and anxiety later in life. Additionally, they seem to be less prone to exhibit signs of mental illness. It seems to sense that people with good friendships frequently feel better, even though mental illness is complicated and friendship cannot take the place of expert care.

- ❖ **Friendship raises confidence**

Their level of healthy self-esteem greatly influences a person's happiness and success in life. Better mental health and stress management are linked to high self-esteem. Any adversity can be overcome by people who are confident in who they are.

Various factors can damage your self-esteem, but strong friendships can restore it. Healthy friends will bolster you when you're down, offer support during trying times, compliment you as a person, not prey on your anxieties, and foster doubt.

❖ Friendship enhances other relationships

Although friendships are only one kind of interaction, they aid in developing social skills that are useful everywhere. As an illustration, it takes effective communication, honesty, and respect to establish a healthy friendship.

These are necessary for relationships in all spheres of life, including romantic, professional, and familial ones. Someone who does not have healthy friendships is probably still engaging in bad behaviors elsewhere. Your other relationships are more likely to be healthy if you keep up solid connections.

❖ Friends make it easier to interact with almost everyone

The circle of friends we choose to have in our life will teach us how to communicate, laugh, and forgive. From our marriage to our workplace, friendship is the cornerstone of every connection. Because of our friends, even those who are different from us or hold a different perspective, we learn how to communicate with people.

We converse with others and learn from them as well. We know the procedure involved in making new friends and learning about their personalities. These people support us in stepping beyond of our comfort zones and provide a safe emotional space for us to be ourselves.

❖ Friends enhance the value of our lives

Our values can be altered by friends, helping us to discover new ways to give our life greater purpose. We saturate our lives with great discussion, genuine care and support, and belly-laughing pleasure when we spend time with friends. Friends are there to aid us and provide perspective while we are struggling.

They grin at our good fortune when we succeed. When we surround ourselves with real, upbeat individuals, we are more likely to practice gratitude and kindness toward others. When we have strong friendships, we don't just survive—we thrive.

Chapter Seven

Keys to Making a True Circle of Friend and a Better Relationship

Friendships are put to the test when times are tough. Your true friends are the ones who stick around once the suffering is done. If you've experienced adversity and lost friends, or if you want more friends, you should be aware of the secrets to a better connection and have a basic grasp of friendships.

1. What transpires with the friends who vanished?

The vanishing "friends" aren't actually pals; perhaps they're only there to take advantage of you when things are going well. They might be there to soak up your happiness and delight. Simply put, they could not care about you as much as you do. Recognize that they cannot be present for you for whatever reason. Assess the value of that expense.

2. Can your buddies be changed?

Your friends can be modified. You can decide to maintain your pals, spend less time with them, put distance between yourself and them, or break up with them. You cannot alter your friend, however. The person is what they are.

3. Are you struggling there?

Life can be difficult at times for almost everyone. It may be a job loss, a loved one's passing, a broken thing, or anything else that makes life challenging. People may not be there for you when your life is difficult if you are not there for them when theirs is. No need to try to come up with the right words; all that has to be uttered is "I am here," and if that proves difficult, simply extend your hand to hold it. Your presence can make a difference even if you can only be there online.

4. Do you rejoice with them?

Celebrate when positive things occur. Hugs and congratulations can be sent to recognize accomplishments. Too frequently, people are reluctant to share their happiness and accomplishments for fear that others will feel envious or would minimize them. The beauty of the moment is diminished by it.

5. Are you reliable?

Being trustworthy extends beyond dealing with things. The foundation of a real friend and improving a relationship is trust. Friends should be able to trust you to honor your commitments. When they aren't there, your friends should have the impression that you will protect them from rumors and won't act rudely. Someone you can trust with your property, partner, feelings, and very existence is a real friend.

6. Are you being polite?

A genuine friend shows respect. Friendships should be treated with respect. Don't alter your circle of friends because you don't want them to change you. Respect them by maintaining your word. Being there with someone in both happiness and grief is essential for better friendships. Celebrate when things start to get better and happier. Celebrate the happiness and your genuine pals.

Signs of A Negative Circle of Friends

Since they have an effect on every part of our life, friendships are essential. Positive circle ones are enlightening, while negative circle ones are harmful. In today's environment, it is increasingly more and harder to sustain meaningful relationships. We observe relationships breaking down all around us, whether they are between a couple, friends, families, or coworkers.

We maintain friendships with people we can trust because of this. However, there are instances when being by yourself is preferable to being with a group of people who only bring you down.

❖ Unreliable listeners are negative friends

In addition, negative circles hardly ever pay attention to your difficulties. Friends communicate their anxieties with one another because they value compassion and support from one another. A poisonous friend would expect you to be there for them when they are down but would be absent when you were in the same situation.

❖ Criticism from negative friends

Additionally, negative friends are overly critical. They are ready to criticize your shortcomings yet become angry when you do the same to them. Continuously negative criticism is the exact opposite of constructive criticism, which can be helpful and even life-changing. Your friend is probably toxic if you feel that you can't talk to them because of their continual criticism.

❖ Unhealthy circles of friend are easily offended

Furthermore, negative friends are likely to act out, either passive-angrily or aggressively. The simplest mistakes cause them to explode or stop speaking with you. You have a bad buddy if you constantly feel guilty or sorry for unimportant things.

❖ Unhealthy Friends resent your accomplishment

When you reach major life milestones, a loyal friend is the first to wish you luck. A poisonous friend is unable and unwilling to share in your joy. They won't acknowledge your achievement.

❖ Negative friends are self-centered

Nothing makes negative pals happier than to brag about themselves. They are the focal point of all conversations. They will ignore you when you attempt to share your life with them.

❖ Negative friends don't stay connected

Even though it's impossible for friends to always talk on the phone, it's important to do so sometimes. A poisonous buddy won't be interested in continuing their friendship with you.

❖ Negative friends disregard your emotions

Also, negative individuals don't take their friends' sentiments into account. They speak without thinking and assume that you won't mind. However, when you step on their toes, they snap easily.

❖ Negative friends exert pressure

Negative circle of friends frequently pushes you outside of your comfort zone for their own benefit rather than yours. While pushing your limits is important, forcing yourself to do so is harmful.

❖ Unreliable friends won't modify their conduct

And finally, a negative circle of friends won't alter their conduct even if it's in your best interests for both of you. They are hindered by pride. Being resistant to development and change is harmful.

❖ Your secrets are never kept

This is among the simplest warning signs of a lousy friend. Don't get us wrong; practically everyone has spilled beans they weren't supposed to at some point. But to constantly be subjected to such by friends? It's untrue. Do you think they won't be able to follow their promises?

Thus, you can't trust them with your secrets? Now that you know this is who they are, you could go out of your way to defend them. But how can you truly expect someone to appreciate you if they can't respect your secrets, a sentimental object that is important to you?

❖ They never acknowledge their errors

Children, preteens, and even teens frequently engage in this activity. Adults occasionally engage in this conduct as well. And as long as it happens occasionally, that's okay. However, if your buddy consistently refuses to take responsibility for their actions, especially when doing so could put you in danger, it may be time to reassess your friendship. How good of friends could they really be if they always put their interests before yours?

❖ They pressure you into taking action

This is one of the unmistakable signs of a toxic social circle. Let's get to it. Nobody has the authority to guilt you into doing something you don't want to do anywhere in the world, aside from your parents.

But if your friends continue to use the one time, they saved you as leverage to force you to do everything they want for the following ten years, that is unquestionably a sign of a lousy friend. Although the idea of reciprocity underlies friendship, it is not founded on guilt or coercion.

- ❖ **You are under a lot of pressure from them**

An overly pessimistic friend will push you to succeed as if you were their lifelong substitute. Overly pessimistic people frequently lack confidence in their own abilities and find it simpler to cling to others. Life is stressful enough without having someone nudge and prod you all the time.

The Secret to Choose Your Circle of Friends

Do you know that you can anticipate your future self five years in advance? You may readily plan your future by knowing your destination, activities, and expected income. The answer is straightforward if you're curious about how: through the company you keep.

Do you know that you can anticipate your future self five years in advance? You may readily plan your future by knowing your destination, activities, and expected income. The answer is straightforward if you're curious about how: through the company you keep. Your personal success is significantly impacted by the people you surround yourself with. Most people's future outcomes may be predicted based just on the company they keep.

Your income is probably in the same ballpark as that of your closest pals. You frequently congregate in the same locations and discuss the same subjects. You can often find that everyone is reading the same books or that no one is reading at all.

When you're prepared to make a beneficial change, you must evaluate your friendships, even if you're best friends with your five closest pals. Relationships are similar to elevators in that they may either take you up or down.

Every relationship isn't supposed to last forever; occasionally, we find ourselves clinging to negative bonds that broke long ago. Making the best decisions in terms of relationships is crucial because of this. You must make the appropriate friends if you want to succeed in the long run. Here are some tips for doing that:

1. Connect higher

Why not be with individuals who are committed to improving their lives, professions, or businesses? Your mind will be opened to many options by doing this. It's normal to feel most at ease around individuals who share your interests and values, and that's fine.

But occasionally, it's beneficial to leave your comfort zone and hang out with pals who can introduce you to larger things, new knowledge, and a higher standard of living. If you cherish these relationships, you will soon see your own progress.

2. Select companions who share your principles

Although variety has many positive aspects, it is best to maintain core friendships with others who share your general values and ideas. Choosing people who share your values will prevent you from compromising or being negatively influenced by individuals who don't uphold your values and the standards that you live by, even though you can appreciate others' thoughts and differences. Friends that have the same ideals can help hold each other accountable.

3. Select friends who share your objectives

These are what I like to call your mission companions. When you have pals that share your objectives, especially if you're an entrepreneur, you may encourage one another. Together, you may work toward your objectives and support one another in doing so.

4. Select friends who can help you balance out your weaknesses

You are aware of your own skills and flaws. We all have them. You can access the talents, skills, and abilities of others who are knowledgeable in fields outside your own with the appropriate friends.

If you have a friend who enjoys organization, but you aren't the best at keeping your closet neat, ask her for help! You might have a writing talent and be able to help a buddy who is revising her resume. Everyone benefits when you play to one other's strengths.

5. Select friends who challenge, inspire, and support you

These pals make excellent purpose partners as well. Nobody likes a friend who is constantly pessimistic or depressed. Typically, the individuals we naturally want to be with are those who are inspiring and upbeat.

What circle do your friends belong to? How do they sound when you speak to them? The best friends will be available to lend a sympathetic ear and assist you in putting a positive spin on any circumstance.

6. Select companions that are like-minded

Friends who share your interests make life more enjoyable. Together, you can take part in activities and excursions. You may go out and do activities with people when you have common interests, whether those are in sports, music, the performing arts, or food. You have a companion with whom you can experience new locations and activities.

7. Pick companions that are eager to learn

Life is about growing, learning, and moving forward. You can learn from each other when you have buddies like them. Having a friend who can provide you with book recommendations or information to aid you on your journey is always helpful. Friends that enjoy reading a lot are typically superb conversationalists and enjoyable to talk to.

8. Select buddies who you can work toward common goals with

You've probably noticed by now that this phrase keeps showing up. To elaborate, a purpose partner is someone you can discuss your dreams and goals with and who will support you in working toward realizing them. Your purpose partners can support you in following through if you let them know what you plan to do. Permit them to check up on you and inquire about your development; reciprocate the favor.

9. Pick friends who will help you celebrate your achievements

You want circle of friends who appreciate you rather than merely put up with you. A true friend will commemorate each milestone, success, and victory along the way. They'll be the first to congratulate you and express genuine happiness at your achievement. Such friends can be hard to come by, so cherish them when you do!

10. Select buddies who have a "get-it" attitude

Get-it folks take their aspirations and accomplishments seriously. They don't take life lightly or frivolously occupy their time. They move quickly and complete tasks. It's crucial to have pals that think and behave in a similar manner if you consider yourself to be a get-it person.

11. Give what you anticipate receiving

Every friendship involves giving and receiving. You must first be a great friend if you want to have wonderful friends. You won't be let down if you follow the Golden Rule and treat people like you want to be treated; you'll find your friendships to be meaningful and rewarding.

Give your connections some thought. Does your circle of friends fit the description above? Can you refer to any of them as your mission partners? If so, that's awesome! If not, it's time to expand and begin forming some new connections. You may improve your relationships' caliber and long-term success by using the tips above.

Ways To Manage Your Circle Of Friends and Have The Best Relationships

It could seem that actions like unfriending, unfollowing, and removing a friend are exclusive to social networking sites like Facebook or Instagram. It's time to trim your friend list and get rid of a few of those alleged "friends" when it grows a little too big. Simply unfollow that friend to stop seeing their postings in your newsfeed if they continue sending you messages you don't want to see.

You might want to unfriend or unfollow your friends on a social networking site for various reasons. But did you think about the possibility that you could also need to do this in actual life? You are, as they say, an average of the company you keep.

It may be depressing to consider that some of your circle of friends may not be supporting your efforts to improve yourself. No, this is not just about giving. It also involves you helping your friends become better people. If a friendship isn't helping you move forward, it can even hold you back. Therefore, it might be time to reduce your real-life friend list.

1. Creating a friends list

Your buddies may not be on a list, but you should know them by heart. It's likely that someone has already been degraded from a buddy to an acquaintance if you can't recall them.

Making a list of your circle of friends and assigning each one a label based on how you believe they influence your life is the first step in organizing your pals. These include:

- Friends who are bad influences on you.
- Friends who don't have an impact on you either favorably or adversely.
- Friends who enrich your life, whether by giving or receiving, in some way.

2. Negative companions

Let's face it, many of us have friends that we are aware don't enhance our lives. These are the friends who might cause us trouble or who are displeased with us. Although we occasionally enjoy their company, you already know our friendship will last. It is preferable to avoid your pals if you have any whom you would prefer not to.

3. Amiable Friends

It's exactly perfect—not too hot, not too chilly, just right. These people are pals, yet they're also not. In other words, they just have no noticeable impact on you. Although it could seem harsh to downgrade this kind of friendship, remember that time is limited, and you need to get to know individuals who can positively influence your life and propel you forward, as well as the reverse.

4. The Ideal Companions

The ideal friend's kinds are the last circle of friends to discuss. These individuals make your life better, are dependable, encourage you to learn and grow, and help you progress. You want to keep these people on your friend list. You're actually giving yourself more time to spend with the ones who can direct you toward better things in life by releasing yourself from the other two sorts of friends.

Conclusion

Although it can be daunting, making new acquaintances is undoubtedly rewarding. After all, friends play a significant role in most of our lives. They are the ones with whom we go through life's ups and downs, pleasures and hardships, side by side. Without friends, life wouldn't be the same at all. Without them, we wouldn't be who we are today. You must decide what kind of friends you want to make if you want to make new ones.

You might wish to start journaling about your efforts. You can reward yourself for your efforts later on by reading about your progress. An actual gift from God is a loyal friend. Men have been known to give their life to save their friends.

Therefore, everyone should understand how to select friends and value friendship. If we want our circle of friends to be honest with us, we must also be honest with them. You will continue to form and maintain a social network as long as you live. I hope this book help you in choosing the right circle of friend and I wish you success as you make your decision. Move cautiously. So that you don't feel overwhelmed, take baby steps.

Made in the USA
Columbia, SC
19 September 2022

67080224R00057